Superapologetics

Proving That Genesis 1 Is Not Only True,
but Divinely Inspired

Nathan L. Bauld

WESTBOW
P R E S S®
A DIVISION OF THOMAS NELSON
& ZONDERVAN

WestBow Press books may be ordered through
booksellers or by contacting:

WestBow Press
A Division of Thomas Nelson & Zondervan
1663 Liberty Drive
Bloomington, IN 47403
www.westbowpress.com
1 (866) 928-1240

ISBN: 978-1-5127-7315-6 (sc)
ISBN: 978-1-5127-7316-3 (e)

Library of Congress Control Number: 2017901104

Print information available on the last page.

WestBow Press rev. date: 1/30/2017

About This Book

Although much of Christian apologetics is intended to affirm the truth of the Bible, the very much more difficult and certainly more important challenge is to affirm its Divine Inspiration —that it is in fact the Word of God. After all, even humans tell the truth some of the time! It is the admittedly ambitious goal of this book to provide proof *beyond reasonable doubt* that Genesis 1 is not merely true but God-breathed. If, indeed, it can be proved that Genesis 1 is divinely inspired, it will be self-evident that the same God Who was at work in inspiring Genesis 1 was almost certainly at work in inspiring the entire remainder of the Bible.

Although it may seem to the reader that this task is an impossible one, I urge the skeptical reader (as well as all other readers of this page) to accept his/her own challenge of reading this book and assessing its conclusions.

About the Author

Nathan L. Bauld was born in Clarksburg, WV and graduated from Victory High School in that city. He attended West Virginia University and graduated magna cum laude with a B.S. degree in Chemistry. He then matriculated in graduate school at the University of Illinois in Urbana, Illinois, earning a Ph.D. in chemistry under the direction of Nobel Laureate E.J.Corey. Subsequently, he pursued postdoctoral research at Harvard University under renowned physical-organic chemist Paul D. Bartlett.

After spending a year as Research Chemist at the Rohm and Haas Company in Philadelphia, he accepted a position in the Chemistry Department at the University of Texas at Austin. He retired as Professor Emeritus in 2005, after 44 years of teaching and research. He is the author of more than 130 research papers in refereed chemistry journals.

Nathan is a member of Austin Baptist Church near Austin, Texas where he sometimes teaches classes in Christian apologetics. Nathan is married to the well-known Austin children's book writer and Austin history writer Jane Scoggins Bauld. They have five children, eight grandchildren, and a steadily increasing number of great grandchildren.

Dedication

I dedicate this work to my wife, Jane

I needed all of your wisdom, ideas, and encouragement,

And they were more than enough!

THANK YOU. JANE

Contents

CHAPTER 1

The Theoretical Basis for Superapologetics

Defining and Subdividing Bible Apologetics

Although nearly everyone understands that Bible apologetics is not a field of study in which apologies are made for the Bible and its statements, it is true that much of apologetics merely defends the *plausibility* of biblical statements and deflects criticism of them. However, there are now many stronger cases in which compelling evidence for the truth of ancient Bible statements has become available from modern science. *Therefore we could choose to speak of apologetics as being weak or strong depending upon whether there is or is not (logical/scientific) proof of the truth of the relevant passages.* Incidentally, this proposed classification as weak or strong is not intended to, nor should it be construed to, disparage weak apologetics — indeed most apologetics is necessarily of this latter kind and is critical for the maintenance of Bible reputation. All

1

that may be needed to convert weak into strong apologetics is the passage of time and the collection and interpretation of relevant scientific evidence.

The Challenge

It is of first importance that we realize that there is not just one, but there are two fundamental aspects of the Bible which the Christian advocate is challenged to defend and, hopefully, to prove. The first is, of course, the *truth* of the scriptures. However, the very important second principle is their *divine inspiration.* This recognition is actually crucial because a given Bible statement or passage may be true, and even may be rigorously proven to be true (strong apologetics), but logically this does not necessarily prove its divine inspiration. *Even human beings tell the truth some of the time!* The challenge to demonstrate divine inspiration is the one that uniquely requires the approach that we propose to call superapologetics.

What Is Superapologetics?

When you consider the task as one of directly demonstrating that God Himself inspired the scriptures as a whole or any given scripture individually, the task seems — and possibly is — outright impossible, humanly. However, if we consider the lesser but nearly equivalent task of eliminating the possibility that the Scripture statements were devised by any highly intelligent or even uniquely brilliant human of the time of the ancient scriptures, we may find ourselves with a more manageable challenge. If this can be accomplished, there should be no further need to ask about the truth of the Bible, in its entirety, since Jehovah God tells no lies!

How can this be Done?

The foundational principle of superapologetics is this:

> *If a robust series of closely related, but concrete, specific, and nonintuitive or even counterintuitive (in other words, amazing) Bible facts from an ancient biblical source have only in modern times been found by science to be true, then these accurate but amazing facts should be accepted as having been divinely supplied to the ancient writer.*

In other words, if such a series can be established, it is proposed that no human writer of ancient times, such as Moses, would have been likely to know *any of these facts* and could not even possibly have known *all of the facts* of the entire robust series. In the ideal circumstance, this could be said to prove that the amazing information must have been derived from a superhumanly well-informed, nonhuman source — i.e., it was presumably divinely inspired by God. When we use the word prove, we refer to *proof beyond a reasonable doubt.* When we assert that this procedure is *nearly equivalent* to a direct proof that God Himself supplied this amazingly prescient knowledge, we are simply recognizing that superapologetics identifies the source of the key information as someone or some entity other than a human being on planet Earth who is either omniscient or who was able to observe for himself these prehistoric events. Of course, this would appear to perfectly describe Jehovah.

It should be admitted at the outset that perhaps not many such extensive and powerful examples of this ideal type of series are likely to be found in brief, localized sections of the Bible, at least at the present time and state off knowledge. However, if even one such example of an *extensive series of high quality* can be found, it will be virtually certain that God's voice has definitely spoken clearly and decisively in the Bible. If that, in turn, is true, is it not appropriate to consider it highly likely that God has protected the entirety of His Word from being corrupted? In other words, that the entire Bible is the divinely inspired Word of God? We are fully convinced that at least one example that rigorously conforms to the standard specifications described for superapologetics is available in the very first book and chapter of the Bible. It is, perhaps, highly significant that in the very first chapter of the very first book of the Bible, proof is supplied of the truth and the divine inspiration of the whole Bible.

Acknowledgment

Before detailing what we consider to be the paradigm example of superapologetics, it is important to acknowledge the groundbreaking work of Dr. Hugh Ross and the Reasons to Believe Institute. The great majority of the factual elements to be discussed here have already been individually identified, analyzed and rationalized by Dr. Ross, and we have used his logic and arguments freely and extensively in this account, with appropriate citations. *If there is any value to the concept of superapologetics, Dr. Ross must be and here is recognized as the pioneer of the fundamental approach to Bible apologetics that is the basis for the proposed concept of superapologetics.* The approach discussed in this text is based simply upon selecting and linking these individual elements tightly together and realizing and asserting that, taken together, they provide a highly logical route to a proof of the divine inspiration of the Bible. We assert that this proof is beyond reasonable (that is, logical) doubt and we apply the new term *superapologetics*. Finally, it is understood that the proof is only indirect in the sense that, fundamentally, it merely excludes a human source of the critical paradigm elements. However, the implication is strong that the source of the information must be divine in order to be able to supply this kind of amazingly correct information.

It is also necessary to point out that some of the interpretations of Bible statements presented in this book are our own, and the responsibility for these interpretations rests solely upon the author of this book and not upon Hugh Ross

CHAPTER 2

The Pillars and Supports of Superapologetics, 1

Supernatural Insights from the Biblical Account of Cosmic Creation

In this Chapter we begin to identify the individual fact declarations of Genesis 1 which are regarded as highly unlikely to have been known to any human of that time but which have been strongly confirmed by modern science. We have chosen to designate these amazing fact declarations as *pillars*, and there are ten of them in all.

Pillar I. The Cosmos Had a Single Beginning of Everything In It, and Genesis 1:1 Is Amazingly Correct in Describing It

The astounding prescience of Genesis 1:1 is far too often overlooked. Hugh Ross deserves much credit for pointing out the amazingly extensive informational content of this verse, but we would like here to focus primarily upon the main thrust of the verse as it refers to the first foundational element or pillar of the paradigm example of superapologetics. [1,2] We note here that all bible verses quoted in this book are from the New American Standard Version (NAS).

In the beginning God created the heavens and the Earth. (Gen. 1:1)

The thrust is clearly that this cosmos *had a beginning — it was not eternally existent.* It seems impossible to deny that this statement is counterintuitive. For millennia scientific icons and the scientific community sharply contradicted this biblical assertion and chose to believe that the cosmos was eternally existing — i.e., that *it had no beginning.*

Aristotle in the fourth century BC,[3] Sir Isaac Newton in the seventeenth century AD,[4] Immanuel Kant in the eighteenth century,[5] and even Albert Einstein in the twentieth century,[6] all considered the cosmos to be eternal. It was not only these eminent scientific and philosophical icons who espoused that theory, but the scientific community in general was equally committed to it. According to this long-reigning theory the cosmos was also considered to be *static* — i.e., the galaxies had always been present and the distances and relationships between the galaxies remained at least approximately as they had always been.

Although Aristotle considered the cosmos to be finite in extent, both Newton and Kant considered it to be infinitely large, as did Einstein —at least prior to his work on the general theory of relativity. So the *eternal, static cosmos theory* reigned in the minds of scientists in general for over two millennia, until after the middle of the twentieth century.

About Einstein

It is an oft-told story, but it must be related here very briefly because it so forcefully illustrates how deeply committed the scientific community was to the eternal, static cosmos theory. At the time —1917 — of development of his field equations of general relativity, Einstein, though he could not solve the equations of general relativity in closed form, was able to discern that they were pointing to an expanding cosmos. He realized that this was inconsistent with a static cosmos and very probably with an eternal cosmos. So, to counteract this, he arbitrarily inserted a constant into his equations which would precisely cancel the expansive tendency. Of course, he later greatly regretted this, but surprisingly the constant now remains in these equations and is called the cosmological constant. However, the constant has a different value and is important in understanding the tendency of the cosmos to keep on expanding and even expanding at an accelerated rate.

The Big Bang Theory

As noted, the idea of an expanding cosmos was already implicit in the original equations of general relativity. However, in the decade of the 1920's, strong experimental evidence was generated in support of this thesis by astronomers LeMaitre and Hubble.[7,8] The discovery of the cosmic microwave background (CMB) radiation, resulting from the initial powerful inflation of the cosmos, by Arno and Penzias in 1965 confirmed and imparted powerful impetus to the theory.[9] From this point forward, the testing and acceptance of the so-called big bang theory was virtually inevitable.

This first biblical pillar, then, provides what should be seen as very strong support for the conclusion that the biblical description of the cosmos as having a temporal beginning would most logically have been provided by a nonhuman source and thus most likely by a divine source. If indeed the description of the origin of the cosmos contained in Genesis 1 is considered to be from a human source, we should ask ourselves *"Is it merely a coincidence that this astonishing information was supplied by a man who was a prophet of Jehovah God?"*

About Other Ancient Creation Accounts

It is perhaps important to note that other ancient creation accounts do exist, such as the Enuma Elish from

Nineveh in the seventh century BC.[9] The question must then be asked *Does the existence of other creation accounts not challenge the assertion that no human being of the time of writing of Genesis 1 would have proposed that this is a created cosmos?*

First, we should note that Moses lived and wrote in the fourteenth century BC, several centuries before the date of the Enuma Elish.[10] The latter, which is the least fantastic and most realistic and detailed of the ancient creation stories, might then have been a derivative of the biblical story.

Second, and of even greater significance, it is not merely the notion of a creation *per se* which qualifies Genesis 1:1 a pillar of superapologetics, but the quality of its creation account and its affirmation in modern science. Whereas many aspects of the Enuma Elish are fantastic and erroneous, it is clear that the unique power of the biblical account is that it proves to be the *true and inerrant story*, as will be seen in the following sections.

Pillar II. The Cosmos Is Not Static, But Has a Dynamic of Expansion!

Once again, much credit is due to Hugh Ross and the Reasons to Believe Institute for the research which reveals that millennia ago the Bible anticipated the expanding or inflationary nature of this cosmos, as is now affirmed by the big bang theory.[1,2] Here are some of the many Bible verses which indicate that the cosmos had an expansive beginning:

- It is He -----who *stretches out the heavens* like a curtain and *spreads them out* like a tent to dwell in. (Isa. 40:22)
- Covering Yourself with light as with a cloak, *stretching out heaven* like a tent curtain." (Ps 104:2).
- Who alone *stretches out the heavens* ... (Job 9:8)
- It is He who made the Earth by His power; Who established the world by His wisdom; and by His understanding He has *stretched out the heavens* (Jer 10:12).
- Thus declares the Lord who *stretches out the heavens*, ... (Zech 12:1)

These are only some of the many verses which describe this cosmos as an expanding one. Ross has cited at least 11 verses by 5 different prophets which describe the cosmos as expansionary.[11] It thus becomes clear that the cosmos was not "popped into" existence instantaneously with fully established galaxies in an "as is" relationship, but that it was expanded or stretched out from a much smaller beginning. *The use of the Hebrew verb tense for continuing action in some of these verses further suggests that, as science now knows, the expansion is still continuing.*

That these verses reveal a radical insight into the origin of this cosmos that is likely of nonhuman origin is again decisively supported by the opposite and antagonistic beliefs of the science community for thousands of years. Specifically, the same scientific icons as well as the scientific community very generally confidently believed over millennia that this cosmos was static, i.e., that the galaxies had always existed, were always infinitely large, and were not moving apart, as we now realize they are certainly doing.

Supports

There are two additional, relevant observations concerning the cosmic creation event described in Genesis 1:1 that we should mention here. We have chosen not to include these observations among the defining elements (pillars) of superapologetics because they appear to be somewhat — but only somewhat— less clearly definitive and concrete than the other insights. Nevertheless, they do appear to provide significant further support for the proposal that the Genesis account provides truths that are unlikely to have human origin.

Support I. The Cosmos Had a Single Origination Of Everything In It

It appears only reasonable to conclude from Genesis 1:1 that this verse is describing a **single origination** of this cosmos, as is specified in the big bang theory. First, the verse grammatically indicates a single beginning (use of the singular of beginning) of all things, not a series of beginnings or even a gradual, continuous inputting of various necessary items in the cosmos. Second, It is implicit in the verse that *everything* in this cosmos originated instantaneously in that singular origin moment. This conclusion follows from the fact that both Hebrew and Christian scholars see the phrase "the heavens and the Earth" in 1:1 as referring to everything in this cosmos, including matter, energy, space, time, gravity, the governing physical laws, and any other force or substance that we do not presently recognize. All of these had their origin in that sudden moment of creation.[12]

This, for example, would have immediately excluded the theory which, in the mid-twentieth century, proposed that the cosmos was indeed eternal but was expanding because of the continuous input of matter and energy into the cosmos.[13] Subsequent to the testing and affirmation of the big bang theory, the steady state theory was virtually completely abandoned.

Support II. The Cosmos Had a Miniscule Origin

The Bible also anticipates the same infinitesimally small beginning of the cosmos that is postulated in the big bang theory. Although indirect, it provides another instance of radical insight into the origin of the cosmos.

> By faith we understand that the worlds were prepared by the word of God, so that what is seen was not made out of things which are visible. (Hebrews 11:3)

Since Bible truth anticipates that this is an expanding cosmos, it follows that at an earlier cosmic time this cosmos was expanded from a state that previously had been much smaller. Logically —by extrapolation — this suggests the possibility that the cosmos may have had a truly miniscule beginning. If we combine this understanding with that of Hebrews 11:3, we may reason that the beginning was *invisibly small.* That is exactly what big bang theory concludes. At the very least, these two supplementary observations contained in 1:1 are nicely compatible with the modern theory of cosmic creation. Surely, this could not have been devised by human intelligence in those ancient times.

In the next chapter we will resume the inventory of the fundamental pillars of the paradigm example of the superapologetic concept and describe many more amazing Bible retroprophecies —prophesies of past, unobserved events— from Genesis 1. These will all refer to the early stages of developments on planet Earth, beginning with Genesis 1:2.

CHAPTER 3

The Pillars and Supports of Superapologetics, II

Supernatural Insights from the Early Developments on Planet Earth as Described In Genesis 1

The series of observations which is intended to anchor the concept of superapologetics began with Genesis 1:1 and now resumes beginning with 1:2 and the following verses which give an account of some of the early creative developments on planet Earth.

The Earth was formless and void, and darkness was over the surface of the deep, and the Spirit of God was moving over the surface of the waters. *(Gen 1:2)*

In this single verse, three rather amazingly specific and concrete facts are declared about planet Earth.

1. There once existed a primordial Earth — i.e., a planet in the beginning stages of formation.
2. Primordial Earth was dark at its surface.
3. Primordial Earth was covered with water.

Pillar III: There Was a Primordial Earth, and It Is Factually and Correctly Described!

The description of Earth as formless and void clearly characterizes the planet as in a primordial stage of development. Let us recall that for thousands of years the principal scientific icons (Aristotle, Newton, Einstein) and the science establishment — when one began to exist— believed that the cosmos was eternal and static. It was not a rational impulse of science or humans that the cosmos or planet Earth had a primordial stage of development at all. We might ask "Why would anyone not simply assume that the Earth had always existed pretty much as it was at the time of the writing of Genesis 1?" The understanding that a primordial Earth existed and the uncanny ability to describe its development in concrete terms is more than just a little impressive!

With the development of the big bang theory of cosmic creation (or the updated standard model of cosmology), it became well established that both the cosmos and planet Earth (of course, at different times) had primordial beginnings and subsequent development.

Pillar IV. The New Planet Was Dark at Its Surface!

The further description of primordial planet Earth as being dark at its surface is not only specific, but bold, and subject to test and potential falsification; we will see that it also turns out to be quite accurate. There was no human or scientific precedent at the time for believing that planet Earth had had no light at its surface. As others —and most especially Hugh Ross — have noted, planetesimals — forming planets— are now known to be typically dark at their surfaces because they are in the process of being formed by the slow accretion of an extremely dense cloud of solid, liquid, and gaseous materials present in their solar systems.[14] Both gravitational and electrostatic forces attract *some* of these substances to the surface of the newly forming planet. However, the surrounding atmosphere is still dense and dark, therefore *opaque*. The early foresight of Genesis 1:2 in this regard is no less than astounding.

Pillar V. The New Planet Was Completely Covered with Water!

The strong implication of Gen 1:2 is that the planet was completely covered with water in its primordial state. However, this is made very explicit later in Genesis 1:

Then God said, "Let the waters below the heavens be gathered into one place, and *let the dry land appear.* (Gen 1:9)

It is certainly a bold and non-intuitive assertion, and there would have been no body of human thought or evidence pointing to this flat declaration by an ancient source. Yet, modern science now affirms the virtual certainty of this aqueous condition. [15,16]

First, it is now known that hydrogen is by far the most common atom in the cosmos and, after helium, oxygen is the third most common. Since hydrogen and oxygen combine readily to produce water, the abundance of water on planet Earth is hardly surprising. More specifically, astronomers have ascertained that planetesimals typically are covered by water in their initial stages.[15] Finally, there is now geological evidence for the strong likelihood that planet Earth in particular was indeed covered with water in its primordial state.[16] In particular, there is evidence that a primordial ocean had already formed as early as 4.4 ba (billion years ago) and that it soon covered the entire planet.[15]

The combination of these descriptions which specify that planet Earth had a primordial stage and that it was dark and covered with water are stunningly accurate!

Pillar VI. Light Came to the Surface of Planet Earth, But the Sun Could Not Yet Be Seen!

Now, in 1:3, we see the statement that at some point in the development of planet Earth, light appeared.

Then God said, "Let there be light; and there was light. (Gen 1:3)

The use of the word *then* indicates that at first Earth was dark and then later, at some point, light appeared. Since the vantage point of the observer had been shifted in 1:2 to the surface of the Earth, the meaning of the biblical statement is that light appeared at the surface of the Earth. As modern science now sees it, it was inevitable that the dense clouds of materials present in primordial Earth's atmosphere would thin out sufficiently for the light of the sun to be seen. Some of these substances would have gradually been attracted to Earth gravitationally and electrostatically and others would have floated off into interplanetary space.

Since planets develop in conjunction with their respective stars, it is highly likely that the sun would already have been in place at the time of primordial Earth. In Genesis 1:3, the light of the sun finally penetrates the Earth's cloudy and darkly opaque atmosphere, and the latter becomes translucent. It would have been the case that the sun and moon could not yet be seen, but day and night were differentiated for the first time.

It is quite important to note that, in effect, Genesis 1:3 does more than declare that light appeared at the surface of planet Earth. Since the sun did not become visible until the fifth day, the full declaration is in effect that *light appeared on planet Earth, but the sun and moon were not yet visible*. This appears to us as a very specific and distinctive description and one which is uniquely compatible with the present day scientific formulation of planet formation, but would have by no means been evident in the time of writing of Genesis 1.

As indicated previously, it appears highly likely that this was not the time when light was created. Radiation, of which visible light is one form, was undoubtedly created in the first creation moment of Genesis 1:1, when *everything* in the cosmos was created. Further, the Hebrew word translated as "be" in the Gen 1:3 statement (haya) means to appear or to happen or to be. It does not mean to create (bara') or make (asa).

While it may not have been so surprising that a thoughtful observer, knowing that the Earth was initially dark, could have surmised that the Earth eventually would have received light, it is noteworthy that *the observer also apparently knew that the sun and the moon were not yet visible*. It is for this reason especially that we have included Gen 1:3 as one of the Pillars of superapologetics.

Nathan L. Bauld

Pillar VII: Earth's Atmosphere Separated. The New Planet Developed a Troposphere and a Water Cycle!

The next event described in Genesis 1, after the arrival of light on the Earth's surface, is the development of an independent, space-limited, watery surrounding atmosphere for planet Earth that was separate and distinct from the remaining interplanetary and other planetary clouds of space debris and moisture in the solar system.

Then God said, "Let there be an expanse in the midst of the waters, and let it separate the waters from the waters." God made the expanse, and separated the waters which were below the expanse from the waters which were above the expanse; and it was so. God called the expanse heaven. (Gen 1:6-8)

Up to this time, clouds of water and space debris still surrounded planet Earth and presumably extended over the remainder of the planets of the solar system. The author of these verses realizes, again very presciently, that planet Earth would soon need to have its own independent and relatively stable atmosphere, separate from the extensive interplanetary clouds and the similar clouds surrounding other planets. This would be essential for the development of plant and animal life that would soon follow. Separating the expanse — or heaven or firmament— from the waters below —the oceans — would require the condensation of more water into the seas, and separating the heavens from the waters above would require that some water move out into other regions of interplanetary space and some to move into the heavens and the seas. *Eventually, the primordial skies would separate out and become distinct from the interplanetary clouds.*

It therefore appears reasonable to construe the expanse or heaven that is immediately above the waters as planet Earth's atmosphere. The waters above the heavens would then correspond to everything in the solar system and cosmos outside of Earth's atmosphere. This is consistent with the ancient Hebrews' view of the three heavens, with the third heaven being the place of God's abode, as indicated by the apostle Paul (2 Cor 12:2). The first heaven is the dome of visible sky as viewed from planet Earth, and the second heaven is the cosmos beyond Earth's atmosphere. *The key point is that the Earth's atmosphere is here separated out from the rest of interplanetary space and the rest of the cosmos.*

Ross has suggested that the expanse or heavens could correspond to the Earth's troposphere, which would be essential for providing for a rain cycle, once land was uplifted and plants began to grow.[17] The waters above the heavens could then correspond to the stratosphere or to the rest of the cosmos. This is an attractive proposal, but we prefer to leave the assignment of the heavens to be more generally the Earth's full atmosphere. *In either case, the understanding by an ancient observer that a distinct, independent atmosphere for planet Earth would be an essential precursor for the development of plant and animal life is worthy of nomination as a founding element of superapologetics.*

Pillar VIII: Dry Land Appeared on the New Planet as a Single Continental Land Mass!

In Genesis 1:9, the first appearance of dry land on the surface of the Earth is described.

Then God said, "Let the waters below the heavens be gathered into one place, and let the dry land appear"; and it was so. (Gen 1:9)

The manner of the appearance of land as described here is what is especially noteworthy. Continents almost certainly did not initially appear in various locations as they now are constituted, but originated in a *single parent land mass*. The ancient writer seems to know, and boldly and concretely expresses, the exact manner in which dry land first appeared on planet Earth. Science now generally agrees that all of the presently existing continents probably derived from a single land mass through a process of volcanism and plate tectonics.[18]

Summary.

A logical analysis of these uncannily correct —as confirmed by contemporary science — and relatively specific descriptions of developmental events on planet Earth would suggest that it is highly unlikely that any ancient human such as Moses would, based on his own human intelligence and intuition, have known any of the six descriptors mentioned in this chapter, much less all six of them. They are specific and concrete descriptors which are susceptible of testing and falsification — if untrue — and they have been tested and found to be highly consistent with modern science. Based upon these six primary descriptors alone, it would appear beyond *reasonable* doubt that the information must have been supplied by a superhumanly well-informed, nonhuman, i.e., divine source. *Further, if it is considered that a human being could have independently known all of these things, is it merely just another coincidence that this particular human being happened to be God's prophet for the nation of Israel?*

CHAPTER 4

The Pillars and Supports of Superapologetics, III

Superhuman Insight into The Origin of Plants, Animals, and Humans

Support III. The Earth Developed a Transparent Atmosphere; The Sun Could Be Seen

The development of a transparent atmosphere on the fourth day logically and scientifically follows the earlier developments on Earth, including the appearance of light, the formation of an atmosphere, the appearance of land and the beginnings of plant growth. It was on the fourth day or epoch that the sun and the moon finally became visible, as would have been expected —from the modern scientific perspective— from the progressive thinning out of the Earth's atmosphere, i.e., a continuation of the same process by which the originally opaque atmosphere became translucent and the Earth's unique atmosphere was developed. Increased sunlight would have encouraged even stronger plant growth and, in turn, this would have converted more of the atmospheric carbon dioxide to oxygen, as would be needed for the survival and proliferation of higher life forms which would follow on the fifth and sixth days.

Incidentally, verse 1:14 specifies that God said "Let there *be* lights in the expanse of the heavens to separate the day from the night." Again, as in the case of the first appearance of light in 1:3, the verb *haya* does not describe a creation but an appearing, for the Earth would not have had primordial existence without its accompanying sun. When, in 1:16, the word *asa* indicates that God *made* the two great lights, it is again not a creation that is being described. Even more importantly, the Hebrew verb translated as *made* is in the verb tense for completed action. It has been well documented that, in ancient Hebrew, which afforded only limited verb tenses, this could have referred to completion at any past time, e.g., it could just as well have been translated as "God *had made* the two great lights". It was finished work already at the time of the observation of a transparent atmosphere. *The pre-existence of the sun and the moon is now mentioned in the narrative because at this stage of Earth's development they had become visible for the first time.* The continuing gravitational accretion of atmospheric particles to the planet's surface and the escape of others into interplanetary space would have continued the thinning of Earth's previously *translucent* atmosphere until at last it became *transparent.*

This explanation, involving the appearance but *not* the creation of the sun and moon, also explains how plants had already been growing on the third day. The translucent light was sufficient for many plants to grow. This insight removes the potential problem of the sun and moon not being mentioned until the fourth day. The logic of this long series of events is now made clear to the modern reader, especially through the insights and efforts of Dr. Hugh Ross.[19]

Support IV. The Long Sequence of Progressive Developmental Events on Earth from Light to Humans is Logically and Correctly Described

Since plants would have required at least some sunlight, it is logically appropriate that, at the first origin of plants, the Earth's original opaque atmosphere had already become translucent ("Let there be light") in Genesis 1:2. Next, the essential water cycle had already been established in the formation of a unique and stable atmosphere to provide for the global distribution of rain. Third, dry land had been uplifted as a medium for plant growth. It is evident that this long series of events leading up to the origin of plant life is eminently logical. It would seem highly doubtful, however, that an ancient human would have been able to reason out such a sequence of progressive developments.

Next, the development of a transparent atmosphere when the sun became visible would be needed to encourage stronger plant growth. This, in turn would convert much of the carbon dioxide present in early Earth's atmosphere to oxygen, which would be needed to support animal life. Earth was then prepared to receive the animal kingdom. As plant life continued to thrive, the oxygen levels would rise even higher and be suitable for the support of human life. The higher oxygen levels would also permit the development of an ozone layer, which would be needed for the survival of higher animals and humans.

Pillar IX. Humans Were the Final Creation. Creations Stopped!

With all of these things in place, the Earth was prepared for the advent of human beings. Not only does the biblical sequence identify humans as the last creation, it further emphasizes the point by declaring that after the creation of humans, God rested (Gen 2:2-3). The latter verse specifies that He rested (ceased) from His *creative works*. It has been clearly established that since the time of creation of man, as established by science, no further kingdoms or phyla have originated. Even the formation of any new *species* is questionable and depends upon the definition of the term *species*, and there are many such definitions in science.

At the very most, speciation now occurs at a glacially slow rate —especially outside the laboratory— as compared to the rate of speciation prior to the advent of humans. The new species, if they are indeed new species and not merely variations of the same species, would almost certainly not have originated by God's fiat creation, but by spontaneous microevolution, that is by very small changes in the species as a result of spontaneous mutation of the DNA. Such mutations have been recognized as potentially producing changes in color or the size of beaks of birds or other small changes that fall short of speciation. Finally, it has been pointed out by Ehrlich and Ehrlich that "It has been more than a century since Charles Darwin started biologists thinking about speciation, and the production of a new animal species in nature has yet to be documented."[20,21]

The question is not whether the biblical reference to the cessation of creations closely models the scientific observations. That is undeniable! The real question is "How could a mere human being have known that the myriads of creations which were ongoing prior to the advent of humans would experience such as a sudden drop-off or cessation?" [21]

Pillar X. All of Present Day Living Humanity Derives from One Specific Man and One Specific Woman!!

Interestingly, God does not specify that on the fifth day the animal kingdom arose from a single pair of individuals of a given species whose subsequent reproduction gave rise to all of the animals of that species. Instead, He says "Let the waters teem with swarms of living creatures." In contrast, Genesis boldly and unequivocally describes humanity as having been derived from the procreation of one single man and one single woman — i.e., Adam and Eve. This retroprophecy is surely astounding in view of both the current and historical views of science.

Until about the decade of the 1990's, the consensus view of science was that different races of humans had derived from different evolutionary processes as a result of differing external conditions on the various continents. In fact, the occurrence of many different races was considered as support for the evolutionary origin of humans. In the view of this theory (the multiregional theory), the different races would have evolved from many different sets of parent humans.

Since that time, however, detailed studies of human DNA from many different regions of the world have conclusively established that all presently living humans in all the regions of the world have derived from a single, specific male (sometimes called Y-chromosomal Adam) and a single specific female (called mitochondrial Eve), in excellent agreement with the fact/prophecy of the ancient manuscript.

Scientists have argued that the DNA studies do not prove that these two individuals mated with each other or even that they were contemporaneous, but that by some means the offspring of other males and females failed to survive and propagate. [22] These considerations, nevertheless, can hardly circumvent the ultimate conclusion that the facts stand in amazing accord with the biblical account and directly contradict the theory of multiregional evolution which was held by most scientists for more than a hundred years.

CHAPTER 5

The Unmentioned and the Unclear

The Unmentioned

Although the Bible obviously does provide some amazingly specific factual accounts of key cosmic creation events and developmental events on planet Earth, it is by no means encyclopedic in its coverage. It is more than obvious that a detailed, continuous account of all of these things would be neither feasible nor comprehensible. *The scriptural coverage is therefore necessarily selective, rather than comprehensive.*

Why Would Things That Appear To Us To Be Important Be Omitted?

Since the Old Testament was conveyed from the writer to the world through a severely limited, ancient form of the Hebrew language, it also appears likely that many phenomena of potential interest simply could not have been conveyed by the writer with sufficient clarity or brevity.

Ancient biblical Hebrew encompasses a vocabulary of approximately one-thousandth of the English language (perhaps only about 6,000 words) and with very limited grammatical forms (only three verb tenses).

Further, as to the human writer of Genesis, it was perhaps not only the minute vocabulary and the primitive grammar of the Hebrew language of the time which would have handicapped him (and any other human of that time) but even more so the absence of contemporary human knowledge of basic concepts and phenomena needed to receive and then convey key aspects of the inspired message. The limitations of both man and language would therefore greatly hinder and even quite possibly prevent many potentially desirable descriptions from being effectively imparted. Of course there would also be the problem of information overload and confusion which might undermine the effectiveness of the text for the wide audience for which it was intended and for the extensive time frame during which it was intended to be operative.

Omission is Not Error

For these and quite possibly many other reasons, it is important to establish the principle that *the omission of events which are known or presumed to have occurred is by no means to be considered a biblical error.* There could have been, and we believe there surely were, good and perfect reasons for including that which was included and omitting that which was omitted. At least some of these reasons almost surely relate to the imperfections of humans and their language and intellectual and emotional abilities and certainly not of any imperfection of God.

Some Significant Omissions

An example of an omission that is sometimes noted is the creation of bacteria, algae, and other microorganisms which science considers to be primitive life forms (but see below). Some are concerned that dinosaurs and hominins aren't given any space. Clearly, however, these phenomena could not have been understood at all until the most recent centuries and their inclusion could have given rise to confusion. Again, the admitted lack of mention of these things and many others should not be and cannot be ascribed to biblical error.

Primitive Life Forms

In verse 1:2, the Scriptures declare that "the Spirit of God was hovering over the surface of the waters", just prior to the appearance of light. First of all this verse appears to alert us to the circumstance that the perspective of the observer in 1:2, which declares the *surface* of the Earth to be dark, and 1:3 where light first appears at the surface, has changed from that in 1:1 where it is logically assumed to be from God's perspective in His heaven. This assumption follows from the circumstance that at the beginning of 1:1 there was no Earth.

Interestingly, the Hebrew word translated as *hovering* in this verse is used only one other time in the Old Testament (Deut 32:11), and in that case it is translated as *brooding*. The biblical context is that of an eagle brooding over or caring for its young. It has been reasonably suggested that the Genesis 1:2 verse could be interpreted as referring to the creation of such primitive life forms as bacteria and algae in the seas of primordial Earth.

What Are 'Life Forms'?

It might be profitable here to pause to consider the differing views that the Bible and modern science have about what constitutes a life form. Scientists classify both plants and bacteria as life forms, although bacteria are termed primitive life forms. The first mention of living or soulish creatures in Genesis 1 is in 1:20, where three types of (apparently) relatively advanced creations (animals) are spoken of — fish, birds, and whales. Unlike science, it appears to us that the Bible does not include either plants or bacteria as life (or soulish) forms.

The Unclear Statements of Genesis 1

We believe that the identification of the pillars of superapologetics, together with several other impressive collateral supports, provide *proof beyond reasonable doubt* that Genesis 1 is the divinely inspired Word of God. There is, however, one other condition which must be satisfied: *If it is truly God's Word, the scriptural passages from which the pillars and supports are derived must contain no demonstrable error or untruth.*

Can Any Statement of Genesis 1 Be Falsified?

It is recognized that Genesis 1 contains a number of additional statements and information beyond those used to define the pillars and the supports. Therefore it would be important to inquire as to whether there are any demonstrably false statements among the range of scriptures from which the pillars and supports are taken, viz., Genesis 1. *In fairly analyzing these other statements, we must affirm the principle that an unclear statement is not necessarily untrue.* Although the truth or falsity of a given statement may be ambiguous or uncertain, it may not be logically concluded to be untrue. To put it another way, there is no burden to prove that these statements are true at any specific point in time; rather, the burden of falsification is to prove that the statements are not and cannot be true.

Why Would God Be Unclear?

Before considering some of these additional statements, we might ask "Why would God be unclear about anything that He wanted to convey?" Referring to the previous discussion of biblically unmentioned but actual historical events, we should understand that both the shortcomings of the ancient Hebrew language and those of the human writer's mind could seriously impede the clear expression of many thoughts or concepts.

The 'Days' of Creation.

One of the potentially troublesome aspects of the Genesis 1 scriptures is the recurring use of the term "day" to describe the seven time periods of the chapter. Whereas science understands that the cosmic origination (creation) event occurred about 13.7 billion years ago (ba), and the age of primordial Earth is about 4.3 ba, the Bible seems to speak in terms of the *days* of creation, numbering them as Day 1, second day, third day, and so on.

However, the Old Testament, including Genesis, contains many passages in which the Hebrew word "yom", translated as *day* in Genesis 1, is obviously, from context, a longer time period than a 24 hour day, including a week, a growing season, a year, a long period of time, and even forever. Consider a few examples:

- This is the account of the heavens and the Earth when they were created, in the *day* that the Lord God made Earth and heaven. (Gen 2:4). The word *day* is a translation of the Hebrew word *yom*. From the context, *yom* refers to the entire creation week just described in Genesis 1. *Yom* therefore actually represents a *week of time.*

- And in the process of *time* it came to pass, that Cain brought of the fruit of the ground an offering unto the Lord.*(*Gen 4:3). *Yom* (actually translated in English as *time, not day*) here refers to a *growing season.*

- ... then let me bear the blame for *ever.* (Gen 43:9). *Yom* (translated as *ever*) represents *eternity.*

- ... to love the Lord thy God, and to walk *ever* in His ways .... (Deut 19:9). *Yom* (ever) represents a *lifetime.*

- In the New Testament, Heb 4:5,6 makes it clear that the seventh *day* is still continuing, and that it still remains for some to enter His Rest.

It also appears that in the ancient Hebrew language of Genesis 1 there was no other word available to specifically describe a long period of time with a definite beginning and ending. The word *olam* could be used to describe a long period of time, but it was used exclusively to describe either an indefinitely long period of time or forever. In either case, it implies the lack of an specific ending.

Some have argued that it is only when the word *yom* is used with an ordinal numeral (like *second day*) that it must mean a 24-hour day. The question of whether the use of the word *yom* in Genesis 1 allows freedom to employ the interpretation of *yom* as an epoch continues to be discussed at length, with many advocates on both sides of the discussion.[23, 24]

In conclusion, as long as the days of Genesis are considered to be epochs, there is no necessary conflict with what are considered to be valid scientific chronologies.

The Creation of Soulish Beings

On Day 5 of the Creation Days of Genesis 1, the scripture states:

Let the waters teem with swarms of living creatures, and let birds fly above the Earth in the open expanse of the heavens. (Gen 1:20).

The phrase often translated as *living creatures* is often also interpreted as *soulish creations*. From the accompanying reference to birds and then later sea monsters (1:21; presumably whales) it is clear that the soulish creatures must be what science classifies as animals. Although these creatures could conceivably be the early, primitive precursors of modern animals which apparently originated *en mass* during the Cambrian Explosion (about 530 ma), it is does not appear plausible to ascribe soulishness to these primitive beings. Further, since they are mentioned in the context of birds, which are a far more modern species than the Cambrian phyla of animals, it would appear to be much more likely that the soulish creatures are, like the birds and whales, more modern animals than the members of the Cambrian explosion. In accord with this reasoning, it is common among biblical interpreters to assume that the soulish creatures are, in fact, primarily fish.

It is relatively well established that both fish and birds experienced a major radiation (increase in population and diversification) during the late Cretaceous and early Paleogene periods (the latter extends from 66-23 ma).[25] It should also be noted that Genesis 1:20 does not specify that the fish and birds were *created* or *made* at this time, but the clear implication is that their numbers and diversity were greatly expanded (radiated) during the time referred to in this verse.

The fifth Day actions, besides fish and birds, also mention the *great sea monsters*, which are usually seen as whales. It is believed that whales could not have originated before the Eocene epoch, which began 56 ma.[26] Consequently, all of the three animal types included in the fifth Day descriptions appear to have arisen and/or radiated (that is underwent great expansion in numbers and diversity) in a similar geologic time frame. The identification of these three animal groups together as *swarming* and *teeming* on the fifth creation day could even be considered as a further example of the amazing and far from obvious or intuitive truths of Genesis 1. By no means can the descriptions of activities on the fifth day be considered as demonstrably false.

Nathan L. Bauld

The Time of Creation of Plants

The biblical account places the creation of plants, including relatively advanced flowering plants — angiosperms— and trees, on the third day (Gen 1:11-13), while the account regarding soulish creatures (including birds and fish) takes place on the fifth day. Since animal life is heterotrophic (meaning animals have to get their food from external sources), while plants are homotrophic (meaning plants can generate their own food), logic requires that primitive plants must have preceded primitive animal life, which presumably would have required plants for food.

However, as noted, the Day 3 account specifies a relatively advanced form of plant life, namely angiosperms, which probably did not appear as early as the most primitive animal forms which arose during the Cambrian explosion (532 ma). Nevertheless, as we have discussed previously, the biblical sequence of plants first and then animals could well be correct if we assume that the soulish creatures of the fifth day are not the most primitive animal forms but more advanced animals like fish and birds and whales. These latter either arose or at least experienced great population and diversity increases (i.e., radiation) in the Paleogene era, which began 66 ma.[26] Specifically, the first angiosperms are considered to have originated about 130 ma, in the early Cretaceous period. Consequently, the biblical chronology of fish, birds, and whales after angiosperms appears quite plausible. It should also be understood that these chronologies give only the minimum age of origin or radiation of the species, and that the survival of remnants of some species (e.g., plants) may be more difficult than for others.

CHAPTER 6

The Power of Superapologetics

The Premises

It is appropriate and important, here in this last chapter, to restate and re-emphasize the premises of the concept of superapologetics.

If a *robust series* of closely related, but concrete, specific, and nonintuitive or even counterintuitive Bible facts from an ancient biblical source have only in modern times been found by science to be true, these accurate but amazing facts, taken all together, should be accepted as having been divinely supplied to the ancient writer.

The Pillars

The series of amazing fact/prophecies which we have proposed to satisfy these specifications are called pillars. Because of their fundamental importance, they are repeated below:

Pillar I. The Cosmos Had a Single Beginning of Everything In It, and It Is Factually and Correctly Described!

Pillar II. The Cosmos Is Not Static, But Has a Dynamic of Expansion!

Pillar III. There Was a Primordial Earth, and It Is Factually and Correctly Described!

Pillar IV. The New Planet Was Dark at Its Surface!

Pillar V. The New Planet Was Completely Covered With Water!

Pillar VI. Light Came to the Surface of Planet Earth, But the Sun Could Not Yet Be Seen!

Pillar VII. Earth's Atmosphere Separated; The New Planet Developed Its Own Troposphere and a Water Cycle.

Pillar VIII. Dry Land Appeared on the New Planet as a Single Continental Land Mass.

*Pillar IX. Humans Were the Final Creation. **Creations Stopped!***

Pillar X. All of Present Day Living Humanity Derives from One Specific Man and One Specific Woman!

The information contained in each of these individual pillars is considered to be so surprisingly prescient and amazingly true, concrete and specific that no human of the early biblical time frame could possibly have known or logically reasoned out the truth described. Each of these pillars is now confirmed by or at least highly consistent with the conclusions of modern science. Taken together, we consider that this robust series of pillars provides evidence beyond reasonable doubt that the information could not have been supplied by any human agency of biblical times.

The Supports

In addition to the foundational pillars of the superapologetic concept, it is also appropriate to take note of still other information contained in Genesis 1 which further tends to affirm the truth of this Scripture, and which we have termed supports. The truth of these supporting statements is perhaps not quite as clearly or as unambiguously demonstrated as in the case of the pillars, but it is considered as lending very significant secondary support to the affirmation of the truth of these passages. A list of these supports is as follows:

> *Support I. The Cosmos Had a Single Origination.*
>
> *Support II. The Cosmos Had a Miniscule Origin*
>
> *Support III. The Earth Developed a Transparent Atmosphere; The Sun Could Be Seen.*
>
> *Support IV. The Long Sequence of Progressive Developmental Events on Earth from Light to Humans. is Logically and Correctly Described*

Beyond Reasonable Doubt

It is understood that *proof beyond reasonable doubt* is not necessarily *absolute proof.* It is anticipated that some or even many will still have doubts. However, we do believe that most reasonable, *unbiased* persons could and should be able accept the fundamental premises of the superapologetic concept and accept Genesis 1 (and thus presumably the entirety of the Bible) as not only true, but divinely inspired and informed truth.

For Those Who May Still Doubt

If someone still insists that, in spite of what we consider to be overwhelming evidence, a human at the time of writing of Genesis 1 could conceivably have independently known and written the facts of Genesis 1, we might ask that person: "Is it merely a coincidence that the one who did know and write these things was a prophet of God?"

The Unique Role of Genesis 1: The Key to Understanding the Divine Inspiration of the Bible

Finally, we find it inspiring and of paramount importance that the Bible opens with a book chapter which strongly affirms its own internal truth and divine inspiration, thereby laying a foundation for understanding that the entire Bible is truly God's Holy Scripture.

References

1. Ross, Hugh, *The Genesis Question*, Navpress, **1998** (First Edition) and **2001** (Second Edition).
2. Ross, Hugh, *Navigating Genesis,* Reasons to Believe Press, **2014**.
3. Aristotle, *On the Heavens*, Translated by J. L. Stock, Book 1, Part 3, Forgotten Books, **2007**.
4. Newton, Isaac, *The General Scholium* in the *Principia,* Second Edition (1713), quoted in a translation by Steffen Ducheyne, *The General Scholium: Some Notes on Newton's Published and Unpublished Endeavours*, **2006,** p 18. [Available on the internet at logica.ugent. be.] *"Since each and every particle of space is always, and each and every indivisible moment of duration is everywhere, certainly the maker and Lord of all things will not be never or nowhere (p.18]".*
5. Kant, Immanuel, *Universal Natural History and Theory of the Heavens;* from *Theories of the Universe, Milton K. Munitz, ed. (Glencoe, IL.; Free Press,* ***1957**), p 240.*
6. Einstein, Albert, *Annalen der Physik*, **49**(1916), 769— 822. English translation: *The Principle of Relativity* by

H.A. Lorentz, A. Einstein, H. Minkowski, and H. Weyl (London: Methuen and Co., 1923), 109—164.

7. LeMaitre, George, *A Homogeneous Universe of Constant Mass and Increasing Radius Accounting for the Radial Velocity of Extra-Galactic Nebulae,* Monthly Notices of the Royal Astronomical Society, **91** (1931), p 483—490.

8. Hubble, Edwin, *A Relation Between Distance and Radial Velocity Among Extra-Galactic Nebulae*, Proceedings of the National Academy of Sciences, **15**, 1929, p 168—173.

9. Van Wolde, Ellen, *Stories of the Beginning: Genesis 1—11 and Other Creation Stories*, translated by John Bowden (Ridgefield, CT: Morehouse Publishing), **1996.**

10. Reference 1, 59—62.

11. Ross, Hugh, *The Creator and the Cosmos* (Third Edition, **2001**), Navpress (Colorado Springs, CO), 24—25.

12. Reference 1, p 18—19.

13. Bondi and Gold, *The Steady-State Theory of the Expanding Universe*, Monthly Notices of the Royal Society, **108** (1948). p 252.

14. Ross, Hugh, *Navigating Genesis*, Reasons to Believe Press, **2014,** p 34—36.

15. Wilde, S.A., Valley, J.W., Peck, W.H. & Graham, C.C., Nature, **409** (6817): 175—178, 2001. Widipedia states as follows: Recent evidence suggests the oceans may have begun forming as early as 4.4 ga. By the start of the Archaean eon they already covered the Earth.

16. Ross, Hugh, *Navigating Genesis,* Reasons to Believe Press, **2014**, p 34—36.

17. Ross, Hugh, *The Genesis Question*, Navpress, **2001** (Second Edition); p 34.

18. Ross, Hugh, *The Genesis Question*, Navpress, **2001** (Second Edition), p 35—36,

19. Ross, Hugh, *Navigating Genesis*, Reasons to Believe Press, **2014**; p 52—54.

20. Ross, Hugh, *Navigating Genesis*, Reasons to Believe Press, **2014**, p 86-87.

21. Ehrlich, P.R. and Ehrlich, A.H. *Extinction: The Causes and Consequences of the Disappearance of Species*, (New York: Ballantine), **1981**, p 23.

22. Ross, Hugh, *Navigating Genesis*, Reasons to Believe Press, **2014**, p 74—75.

23. Norman, Greg, *Old Earth Creation Science*, in Old Earth Ministries, **2005**. Web Address: OldEarth.org

24. Stambaugh, James, *The Meaning of "Day" in Genesis*, Institute for Creation Research: Web Address: icr.org.

25. *Evolution of fish*, Wikipedia; en.m.wikipedia.org

26. *Timeline of the evolutionary history of life*, Wikipedia: en.m.wikipedia.org.

Printed in the United States
By Bookmasters